YOUR
HANDY COMPANION
TO
DEVISING
AND
PHYSICAL THEATRE

By Pilar Orti

Including "Five Plays to Play With" by
Phillip Johnson, Richard Mann,
Pilar Orti and Mark Reid

Your Handy Companion to Devising and Physical Theatre
By Pilar Orti

ISBN: 978-1-4478-5545-3

Published by Paperplay.

CONTENTS

INTRODUCTION

More and more young people are studying physical theatre as part of their Drama programmes. Most qualifications (be they Drama, Theatre Studies, Performing Arts etc) require students to devise their own work. This is often seen by teachers as an opportunity to encourage them to be as theatrical as possible in their approach and steer them away from naturalism. This can sometimes be difficult as young people's performance style is mainly influenced by television. Furthermore, most young people have little exposure to theatre and even when they do watch a live performance, chances are that the acting style will resemble that on the screen, as in a traditional musical theatre show or a "straight play".

I am of course making a broad generalisation but my experience of working with young people in the UK is that most under-16s will have had little exposure to highly theatrical work. Once students are older, teachers find it easier to organise trips to see more adventurous work and the students themselves begin to seek more challenging experiences as an audience.

It is therefore quite difficult sometimes to encourage drama students to use physical theatre in their own work, when they might not have seen the art-form before or when they do not consider it to be "proper acting". It is therefore important to enthuse the students about it by pointing out the ways in which it is different to naturalism and highlighting the advantages of using this style.

The benefits of working with physical theatre are clear to teachers: the imagination is stretched, physical expression is developed and collaboration becomes a necessary part of the devising experience. For the students, the benefits might need to seem more "product-based". For example:

- The story can be "filmic" as the action need not be restricted to the here and now but can take place in different locations, as the need for literal sets is removed;

4

- Being part of an ensemble means that all performers can contribute equally to the piece – there is no need for "main parts";
- Through the use of music and movement, the audience's experience can be made memorable, regardless of the length or complexity of the piece.

I have written this book for both students and teachers.

My aim is to support those drama teachers who, with little experience of physical theatre themselves, have a genuine interest in the style and are keen to enthuse their students to use it in their work. At the same time, I hope the book will prove valuable to those students who are already passionate about the subject and are keen to bring the style into their own work. I can safely say that in every group of drama students, there is always one who will go beyond the call of duty, driven by a genuine interest in all kinds of theatre and a passion to contribute to the art form. If you are this student, this book is for you.

This book consists of four parts.

Part 1: DEVISING AND PHYSICAL THEATRE could be viewed as an advocacy document, highlighting the joys of physical theatre and ensemble work.

Part 2: CREATING PHYSICAL THEATRE begins with a suggested structure for the devising process, for those students who need to create a piece for their assessment. This is followed by a small number of exercises to help with building the ensemble, creating a character and story and using theatrical devices. Many examination boards require the teachers to have as little input into the devising process as possible. Guidance is, of course, accepted, as is feedback on the material as it is created. For this reason, I have written the instructions to the exercises in part two, with the *students* in mind. In this way, if a teacher wants to use them in class, they can; or if they want to photocopy them and give them to the students for *them* to incorporate them into their sessions, they can do so too.

If as a teacher, you use the exercises on Creating a Character with your students, you can also take the opportunity to raise their physical and emotional self-awareness, debriefing each exercise by asking questions like "How did that make you feel?", "What movement was easier/more difficult to do?" etc.

Part 3: WORKING WITH MASKS introduces mask work. While this is not something that will be tackled by everyone, it is worth considering as an option. For students, it might allow them to create a large number of characters if their piece requires it. For teachers, using masks during exploration can help to illustrate focus, simplicity of movement and honesty in performance.

"Whatever its dramatic style, all theatre profits from the experience an actor gains through masked performance. This is an example of teaching which does not operate directly, but through a ricochet effect."
Jacques Lecoq in 'The Moving Body'.

The final part of this handbook is made up of five scripts that have been used to explore physical theatre. The pieces were created by members of Forbidden Theatre Company's ensemble and presented during their Freestyle Performances. Some of the pieces will seem more polished than others but all of them illustrate how working in a stylised way can take the audience to a different world.

This is by no means the authoritative guide to physical theatre or a thick volume of exercises (I have included a list of books at the end that will fulfill that function). It is a reminder of the ways in which physical theatre can be used to nurture the imagination and sense of collaboration in drama students. I hope it will be of use.

Do feel free to leave your comments on the blog:
http://devisingandphysicaltheatre.wordpress.com

Let us know what worked for you and your students.

Pilar Orti

July 2011

PART 1
DEVISING AND PHYSICAL THEATRE

"I often tell actors that imagination is in the body: rather than being limited to a space in the brain, it lies in the movements of fingers and toes, in the contraction and relaxation of muscles. In improvisation, imagination is the response of the body to space, time, music and human dynamic that fuels the thinking brain, not the other way around."

Christian Darley, 'The Space to Move'.

CHAPTER 1

INTRODUCTION TO PHYSICAL THEATRE

Our imaginations are boundless. Our lives are surrounded by stories of all kinds: urban myths, fairy tales, stories which are so rooted in real life that we mistake them for the truth. We explain the world around us through myths and stories, even through fables whose characters are not human.

As audiences, we enjoy stretching our imaginations. When creating a piece of theatre therefore, we can allow our imaginations to run free. We do not need to limit our situations to those which are "believable": our characters can travel across rivers, fly or exist in dreams and other surreal places. As humans we crave stories that will take us away from our ordinary world – that is why, despite the birth of film and television, theatre still has an audience today.

Theatre is a celebration of all that is human. The purpose of devising is to create together something which will be unique to each performance group.

Why Use Physical Theatre?

Whatever the stimulus for a devised piece (be it the work of an artist, a well-known story, a newspaper article), there is a need to ensure that the audience is taken on a journey. There might be elements of the story that seem difficult to communicate to an audience because it is difficult to act out their "reality". However, physical theatre can help to communicate the most fantastical or abstract concepts.

For example, by using physical theatre we can:

- Depict fantastical physical journeys. For example, by creating the illusion of traveling through the air (without literally being flown through the space with a rope);

- Create surreal environments (such as somebody's mind);

- Develop characters from another world (such as those that are half human and half animal or grotesque villagers);

- Have flexible, easy to use sets – created by the performers, as they become walls, rivers, furniture, etc.

Through full belief in what they are doing and commitment to the piece, the performers will carry the audience with them.

To clarify the need for using physical theatre, you will need to discuss the desired effects on the audience and encourage the students to evaluate its impact through collaborative discussion and the use of an "outside eye" such as yourself, other tutors or other students.

- If the intention is to convey EMOTION, the movement used can be choreographed, almost dance-like. In this way abstract sequences can be created, intended to make the audience FEEL in a certain way.

- If a human set is needed, the movement used (or stillness) will need to be more literal. For example, to create a wall, rigidity might be needed (or a crumbling movement if it is smashed). If you are depicting furniture, the performers will have to look like the real thing as much as possible.

- If the main aim is for the audience to fully understand the story, then maybe physical theatre might be used to create a range of distinct characters, while keeping their actions realistic. Dialogue and storytelling can help to make the story clear.

These are some examples of how physical theatre can be used when creating a new piece. Before we move to the practicalities of it, we must address the importance of the ensemble.

The Ensemble

Physical Theatre prides itself in creating ensemble pieces, where ALL performers are vital to the piece. Ensemble members work well together, feeding off each other during the creation process, listening on stage to each other with their ears and bodies, in tune with what they are all doing, all the time. When an ensemble is working well together, the audience FEELS the performers' joy in collaborating and this in turn heightens the audience's experience.

Working well as an ensemble does not necessarily mean that everyone gets on incredibly well all the time and that they are all great friends. It means people respect each other, share a common theatrical language and believe in what they are creating together. It is very important therefore that performers warm up together before rehearsals, carry out games and exercises to increase awareness of each other and spend as much time as possible trying out ideas in the space. Only in this way will they really understand how they operate individually and as a group.

It is always worth reminding students that the ensemble is made up of individuals and as such, everyone needs to take responsibility for their role in the creative process. Everyone works in different ways - understanding how this enriches the piece, will make the work even better. On a practical level, the ensemble needs to take care of the whole piece while the individual is responsible for developing his/her own character/s and bringing emotional truth to them. It is worth pointing out that although students might have great ideas about how others' characters should be developed it is important that each performer explores their own ideas first, as long as they are within the constraints of the piece and story. This will hopefully remind the more vocal students that this is the chance for everyone to take ownership of the piece.

CHAPTER 2
STRUCTURING THE DEVISING PROCESS

The creation of a new piece will be a roller coaster: some days enormous amounts of material worth keeping will be created, while other days everything created will seem useless. Remind students not to give up, not to be discouraged as this is all part of the creative process! It is precisely through creating material that does not seem to work which will help define more clearly where the piece is going. Sometimes it is just as important to discover what does not work as it is to create material that does work.

Usually students will have a long time during which to develop a piece (usually in short, sporadic lessons over 10 weeks). This is good news: it means they can experiment with ideas, dedicate sessions to developing character, incorporate the research gradually into the piece... you name it. But in order to keep the process fluid and give themselves room to experiment and play, they need to be extremely well organised.

The first thing to encourage is to set themselves some <u>deadlines</u> for the completion of the practical aspects of devising, such as the costume and set designs and a written script for the sound and light operator. Ask the students to set some deadlines and stick to them – after investing all their creativity in the piece, they probably do not want the practicalities of theatre to get in the way of their greatest enjoyment: the performance.

Below is a suggested structure for the devising process. Different groups work at different speeds. Depending on the stimulus, they might need to allocate more time to some sections than I suggest here, so make sure they only use the suggested structure as a guideline. In any case, remind them to use their time **together** productively. It is no use allocating a lesson to character development, where everyone sits down and writes their character profile individually, when this could be done at home.

Remind them that their time together as an **ensemble** is incredibly valuable and limited. Similarly, ask them to use their contact time with you and other tutors wisely. If they show you a section of the work during one lesson, they must make sure the next time they ask you to watch their piece, that section has been developed further.

If the students need a script for their lights and sound operator but there is little or no dialogue, they will need to describe what is happening on stage and how the plot is advancing. If there are specific visual moments to act as cues for lights and/or sound, remind them to describe them in detail in their script.

Below is a structure and timeline that you might need to share with your students. If it is likely to need modifications to suit your own schedule, amend it with them. It will be a good exercise for them to start getting their heads around what the whole process will involve.

The Devising process can be divided into three stages, which will probably overlap.

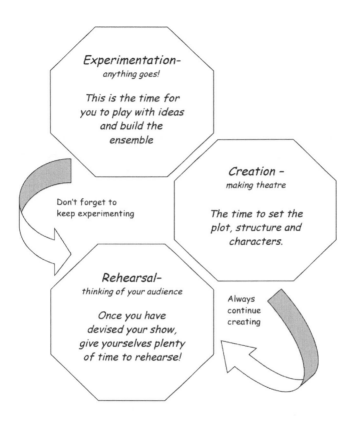

Experimentation-
anything goes!

This is the time for you to play with ideas and build the ensemble

Creation –
making theatre

The time to set the plot, structure and characters.

Don't forget to keep experimenting

Rehearsal-
thinking of your audience

Once you have devised your show, give yourselves plenty of time to rehearse!

Always continue creating

Assuming you have ten weeks to develop your piece, your time might be used in the following way:

Week 1

*Improvisations around stimulus. Research on stimulus (if appropriate). Decide on style. Building the ensemble. Discuss creating and rehearsal process. Do as much research as you can during the first three weeks of the process. This is the time where you are likely to be experimenting and therefore not needing to do much work on the piece itself in between rehearsals, such as learning lines. Once you have decided on the theme/s likely to appear in your piece, research them and make sure you allocate time to **share** your findings. Also, do not forget to look into which theatre practitioners are likely to influence you. Again, you will need to research their work.*

Week 2

Share your research. Decide on where the piece is going. Maybe the full storyline. Maybe a strong definition of characters. Begin research on themes.

Week 3

Continue improvising. Individual character work. Character profiles. Research on practitioners suited to the piece.

Week 4

Set the story line and outline of the piece. Begin CREATING the piece. Order of scenes. What happens in each scene. Begin scripting. Start thinking of set and costumes.

Week 5

First drafts of set and costume designs. Continue creating the piece. More character development. Character-led improvisations which will lead to development of plot.

Week 6

Begin rehearsals. Continue Development.

Week 7

Final set and costume designs. Purchase or identify set and costume elements. Continue rehearsing and development. Ask people to be your "outside eye".

Week 8

Rehearsals. Define scene changes (if applicable).

Week 9

Have written down the final script. Run-throughs. More rehearsals.

Week 10

Tech Rehearsal. Dress Rehearsal (x2 if possible) Performance!

Once a schedule has been created, suggest that it is revised at the end of each week. If a group manages to hit on a wonderful storyline on day 2 of Week 1, then maybe they can start detailed character work earlier on so they can give themselves some more rehearsal time. Devising is not only group specific, but project specific too and the process varies continuously.

At the end of Week 1, ask the students to discuss how they envisage carrying out the creation and devising process as a group. Will each member be responsible for a session? Will they want a tutor to run a session on Character Development so that all group members can work on their characters at the same time? Similarly, ask them to discuss who will be running the warm ups for each session. For some sessions they will need longer warm ups than others, but you should encourage them to always do SOMETHING together, even if it is a quick game of tag to get them all making physical contact with each other before beginning each rehearsal.

Just as it is paramount to schedule an exercise to bring everyone together at the beginning of the session, it is vital to wrap up the session too. Five minutes at the end of each session to reflect on what has (or hasn't) been achieved are very useful, as is making sure that everyone agrees on what the next steps of the process are and what shape the next session will take.

Group Preparation

As with all drama workshops or rehearsals, it is essential for the students to warm-up at the start of the session, to get their bodies and minds ready for the work to come. The importance of warming up together through working on the body individually and playing games cannot be emphasised enough. Its benefits go way beyond "getting ready". Here are just some of the reasons why warming up together is essential – some of them apply especially to physical and mask work, but most of them are relevant to all actor training.

- Connecting the body and mind.
- Developing physical and emotional awareness.
- Training spontaneity and "being in the moment".
- Training taking risks.
- Training making mistakes together.
- Practising communicating in ways that don't include words – a look, a smile, a gasp, a laugh.
- Isolation of body parts.
- Warming up of joints.
- Spatial awareness.
- Practising humility, collaboration and commitment.

The list goes on.... For those students that don't like playing games because they want to get on with "proper acting", this list can provide a good reminder of how the exercises will help them to be better performers.

Don't feel like you need to vary your warm ups or play different games each time you begin a session. Practice makes perfect and some of these games become really interesting once everyone is skilled at playing them. This is also a very good way to train the craft of acting: an actor does not change character or script at every rehearsal; the skeleton of the work is the same and it is a skill to be able to explore different things within a tight framework. And once the professional actor is in performance mode, they need to find the freshness of the first performance every single time, through their trained spontaneity.

PART 2

CREATING PHYSICAL THEATRE

"Error is not just acceptable, it is necessary for the continuation of life, provided it is not too great. A large error is a catastrophe; a small error is essential for enhancing existence. Without error, there is no movement. Death follows."

Jacques Lecoq, 'The Moving Body'.

CHAPTER 3
BUILDING THE ENSEMBLE

Here are some of my favorite games. You probably recognise some of them from other drama lessons/workshops or from your childhood.

The Clapping Circle
The performers form a standing circle. One person starts passing one clap to the person on the right, who receives the clap and passes it to the next. As the clap travels through the circle the sound should be that of one person clapping. Once a rhythm has been established, the performers can reverse the direction of the clap or pass it across the circle.

It is important that the performers are centered, standing with their legs at least hip-width apart and that they use the whole of their body when passing the clap. Eye contact with the person they are sending it to is of vital importance. This simple exercise gets the group focused, aware of each other, and listening to the rhythm the group creates.

Grandmother's Footsteps
One performer (the "grandmother") stands facing a wall. Everyone else stands behind him/her at the other side of the room. The object of the game is for the rest of the group to creep behind the grandmother and tap her on the back. The grandmother will turn every few seconds and when she does, everyone must freeze. If she sees anyone move in the slightest, they have to go back to where they started. Whoever reaches the wall, becomes the next grandmother.

This game wakes up the body and mind and, though competitive, encourages performers to work in physical closeness to each other sharing the same space.

Grandmother's footsteps is used widely to teach acting and physical theatre. The game has the added benefit that half of the class can sit and watch. What makes a good piece of drama and what is interesting about watching actors suddenly becomes apparent: enjoyment, commitment, the need to take risks, the need to play within the rules, suspension... this game has all the ingredients of a good theatrical performance.

When we freeze as Grandmother turns, we don't stop: our emotion is in motion. Our brains are ticking away, making sure that every single element of our body is still, we are holding on to our energy, not letting it go... and we are oh-so-ready, because at any point, Grandma will turn round and then..... we have to be ready to move!

Counting to Ten
The group stand, or sit in a circle, with their eyes closed. The aim is to count to ten or a higher number (the number aimed should be higher than the number of people in the exercise). The group must make sure everyone is ready to start the exercise and then someone at random starts by saying "one". Someone else will then say "two" and so on. If two people say a number at the same time, the count must start again.

This is an ideal exercise to focus the energy, to channel it into the group and get everyone listening to each other extremely carefully.

Tag games are good energisers. They also encourage you to move spontaneously in the same space as your fellow performers. Here are some variations:

Name Tag
A game of tag. Someone is "it". When someone is about to be caught, they must shout somebody else's name. That person then immediately becomes "it". If someone is actually caught, they are out.

Hug Tag
Another game of tag. The only way to prevent being caught, is by hugging another person. If someone is caught, they become "it". The space where the game is played should not be very big.

Elves / Witches / Giants

Similar to the traditional "paper, stone, scissors". A physical movement to represent each of the creatures is decided at the beginning of the game. The class then divides into two groups and each decide amongst themselves what group of creatures they are going to be. Elves overpower giants, who overpower witches, who win over elves. The two groups then meet in the centre of the room (between their homes) forming two lines. At the count of three they physicalize their creatures, and those with greater powers have to chase the others, who can save themselves by running to their "home".

19

If any of those with "greater powers" catch someone from the opposite side, they will add them to their team.

The Empty Chair

This game works best with at least 7 people. Distribute evenly the same number of chairs as people playing across the space. Everyone but one person, the Walker, sits on a chair. The empty chair must be at one end and the Walker will start the game at the other end.

The aim of the Walker is to sit on a chair. S/he will do this by walking towards it <u>at an even, slow pace</u>. Everyone else must prevent the Walker from sitting on the empty chair. This is done by leaving their chair and sitting on the empty chair. This will leave another chair empty. The Walker will then try to get to it but someone else from the group should go towards it and sit on it. Everyone but the Walker can move as fast or as slow as they wish.

Note that once a member of the group lifts their bum from their own chair, they can't go back to it and have to sit somewhere else. When the Walker finally sits on a chair, the game ends and whoever was not sitting down, becomes the Walker.

Once you have played this game a few times and are familiar with the strategies that work, try to play the game in silence. Of course there will be cries and laughter but try to avoid communicating with words and avoid telling others what to do. This will help you to develop your ensemble skills, where everyone in the group shares the responsibility of achieving a common goal.

CHAPTER 4
CREATING A CHARACTER

The following exercises can be used during different stages in the devising process to create characters, develop the plot or develop the characters' personalities. You can create a character right at the beginning, before you even have a character profile. You can experiment with the different physicalities developed through the exercises and begin to build your character around the physicality.

Interesting situations often arise out of conflict – this might be between two characters or the inner conflict a character might experience. You can develop your plot by placing your character with the new physicality in a scene. You can then change the physicality in the middle of the scene, and find the psychological reason for this change on your feet, or later as you reflect on the piece or by consulting with an "outside eye". (For more on changing your physicality, see The Seven Levels of Tension.)

If you have assigned your characters a state of tension, you can place them in situations where their state is altered. Allow the performers to develop the reason for the change on their feet, by doing the scene: you might all be surprised by what you come up with.

Once you have a character profile and a character journey, you might want to experiment with these techniques to help you find a way of moving which is different to your own, to develop your character. These techniques can help to fuel your imagination, by encouraging you to move and use the space around you in ways that are not familiar to you, creating a wide range of options for your character.

The Seven Levels of Tension

For the following exercise you will need to increase the tension in your muscles gradually. Make sure you move swiftly from one stage to the next and that you are warmed up before you start. Your warm up should include relaxation and stretching exercises.

Start by lying on the floor. Feel your weight giving in to the floor. You are aiming for a state of complete physical relaxation. As if you'd been doing hours and hours of exercise and you had completely collapsed on the floor. This stage is:

Level 1: **Collapse** - no energy, heavy, every action is a massive effort.

Gradually begin to move your body. Start with a foot, or a finger, until you have slightly more tension in the body. Only enough to get yourself up and have a relaxed walk around the room, maybe imagining it's a nice sunny day and you are walking in the park. You are now at the next state:

Level 2: **Sunday afternoon** - A 'cool' walk, very little energy is used for movement.

Now change your walk so that you reveal as little about your state of mind as possible. Make your pace even, arms swinging casually by your side, straight back, open chest, with no expression on your face. This is the most difficult state to achieve.

Level 3: **Neutral** - No emotion, gives nothing away.

Now pretend that during your walk, you remember you left the oven on. You begin turning back but decide that after all, you *had* switched it off. Then you think about it again and turn back. No, it's definitely off. No maybe it's on… etc. Each time you have a new thought, the body tries to move in a new direction, until your movement is jolty. The body now begins to have more tension than you are probably used to. This is

Level 4: **Confused** - Yes/No, the clown rhythm.

You finally decide that you did indeed leave the oven on and straightaway head home. You are in control, nothing is really going to happen but now that you have decided to go back home, you might as well get there as soon as you can. It is no surprise that this next level is called:

Level 5: *Decide and Go* – Very direct, definite movements. Tension begins to rise in the body, but still controlled.

However as you walk towards your house, you remember that not only did you leave your oven on, but also the washing machine, and the video. Scared that there might be a power surge, you run back home in a state of:

Level 6: *Panic* – A high level of tension in the body now, the movement becomes very fast, in all directions.

The last state is rarely seen in real life. Imagine that the tension during the panic state builds up so much that eventually the muscles are all so tense that you freeze.

Level 7: *Hypertension* – There is so much tension in the body, that movement is impossible. This leads to collapse.

Using the seven levels of tension to develop plot.

To develop your story further, you can place characters in situations and then change their level of tension suddenly. For example, imagine your character is a level 2, very chilled out. We can place him/her in a familiar situation to them, enjoying sitting on a park bench, reading a newspaper, with another character. The level of tension of our chilled out friend suddenly changes to that of Level 6, panic. They've read something in the newspaper that has made them incredibly nervous, or maybe they've heard a series of strange sounds that brings back past unpleasant memories or maybe they've remembered they were angry at the other character for something. All this can be decided by the actor on their feet or they can play the scene and decide on the reason for the change of physicality later.

The Elements

This is a similar exercise to The Seven Levels of Tension. Make sure you move swiftly from one stage to the next and that you warm up before you start. Your warm up should include relaxation and stretching exercises.

Water

Starting from a neutral walk, imagine you come across the edge of the sea. Start going into the water, feeling it under the soles of your feet, then up your ankles, knees etc. Do this gradually, feeling how the movement of your limbs changes when they are under water. There is more resistance than when you walk through air. Carry on until the whole of your body seems immersed under water. Then reverse the process until you are back at neutral.

The movements of very watery characters are fluid, and lacking in angles. Their walks are circular, in curves, not at sharp, straight angles. Water people are very calm and practical. (For positive qualities, think "stream"; for negative, think "floods".)

Air

Imagine your feet start to fill up with air, then your legs, hips etc until even your arms and head seem like they are floating. Your eyes too have air behind them. Try to have a conversation with others – you probably don't get beyond "Hi!". Once you've had enough of the airhead experience, reverse to neutral.

The limbs of airy characters are very light and their movements practically weightless. They are stuck in their own reality, and have their head (almost literally) in the clouds. (Positive: breeze; Negative: hurricane.)

Earth

Always keeping your back as straight at possible, begin to imagine that your feet are very heavy. And so are your legs. Although they are heavy, you can still lift them with no effort, but feel your connection to the ground. Apply the same principle to the rest of the body. Your arms, they are heavy but you can move them, your gestures are probably well defined and direct. What's it like to shake other people's hands?

The movement of earthy characters is very solid, and mostly performed in straight lines, as opposed to the more curved movements of the air/water characters. Their weight is directed downwards (towards the Earth) and steps tend to be grounded but not always heavy. These characters are also practical but can also be aggressive and confrontational. They will hold their ground. (Positive: solid soil; Negative: volcano.)

Fire
After having gone back to neutral, imagine that the ground begins to feel hot. The soles of your feet are burning and you try to reduce the amount of time they are in contact with the floor. The heat sensation starts going up through your legs, and your torso, your arms…. There is even fire behind your eyes…… Make sure you slowly bring this down, and bring yourself back to neutral.

The movements of fiery characters are very erratic. They follow a similar to the yes/no pattern common to the clown. They therefore sometimes appear nervous or insecure. On the other hand their movements are full of an energy which might be dangerous either because of its lack of direction and focus or because of its power. (Positive: warmth; Negative: fire out of control.)

Using The Elements to develop characters.

If you have already started to build your character, you can use The Elements to help you build their physicality. Your character might be quite dippy, in which case the physicality for AIR might be appropriate. There might be things that make them nervous, adding short bursts of fire to their physicality when this happens.

Depending on the style of your piece, you can use these physicalities to varying degrees. A piece with grotesque characters might take a character that moves through the space as WATER very well but if you are using this for more realistic characters they might just have the **qualities** of water. Their speech might be fluid, their walk purposeful but smooth and they might always remain calm in difficult situations.

Grotesque Characters

Your piece might benefit from Grotesque Characters. If you are telling a fantastic story, or have surreal sequences (like dreams) it might be worth exploring how to alter your physicality to create a character that is immediately recognised as out-of-this world.

You can combine the Seven Levels of Tension and the Elements to create odd characters. You can also just use the Elements – giving your upper half the physicality of one element and the lower one the physicality of another one. This can have very comic results.

You might also want to heighten the use of certain body parts. Make sure you move swiftly from one stage to the next and that you warm up before you start. Your warm up should include relaxation and stretching exercises.

Explore one body part at a time:

If you had big feet, how would you walk?

If your knees directed your movement, how would you walk across the space?

What would happen if your bum was the biggest part of your body?

If it was your chest?

What would happen if you had a stiff neck?

And how would you move across the space if your neck was your biggest part?

Experiment with combining two or more of these heightened body parts. Try to perform every day actions like sitting down, lying down on the floor, putting on your clothes, reading a book...

Finding a Voice

When finding a voice for your character, avoid going straight into speech – play first with sounds. This is especially relevant if your character is out-of-this world.

What sounds do they make when they finally sit down after a long day? What do they shout when they miss the bus? You might even try to have a conversation in a nonsensical language first (if you can't think of one, just say "rhubarb rhubarb") and then eventually go into speech.

Character Journeys

If you are struggling to develop the plot of your piece but already have very strong characters, it might be worth looking at your characters' individual stories.

Individually, map out what happens to your character through the piece. What are they doing at the beginning of the piece, how do they feel? And how do they change throughout the piece? In what emotional state are they at the end?

Prepare a short piece to show the rest of the group – lasting no more than two minutes – which <u>shows</u> the character's journey: maybe through still images or by mixing narration with abstract images that show emotions.

This should highlight any gaps in the journey or any moments which are not clear. They might provide you with material to develop into one or more scenes or might even spark off ideas for a subplot.

Swapping Characters

Half way through the devising process, when you feel like you know your own characters inside out, when you are already familiar with the world you are creating, it might be worth taking some time to gain some distance from your own contribution to the piece.

A way of doing this is by swapping characters. You can take scenes that have already been developed or allow yourselves to improvise new material while in another character's shoes.

When you are playing somebody else's character, try to find the essence of that character – avoid mimicking your fellow actor's performance, bring something new to the role.

Debriefing is very important after this exercise – discuss whether you think there are elements in this new interpretation worth incorporating into your character and make sure you bring up anything that strikes you as very different from how you have been playing it. It might be that your fellow actors thinks that new characteristic might work but it might be that what you are playing is communicating to the audience something different from what you intend to portray.

Interactions

This exercise will help you to develop your characters further and begin to interact with other characters. You will need an "outside-eye" to run the exercise and a group of you should form an audience. The audience's role in this is essential, as they will be the ones using their imaginations to make connections between the characters.

In the performance area, set a chair or other object downstage left and downstage right. One chair will signify "very much" and the other one "not at all".

Have three or four characters on stage. The exercise leader will ask questions about the characters. For example, how much does your character love money? The performers will need to position themselves between the chairs, depending on whether they are closer to "very much" or "not at all".

How much do you love money?

How much do you like working?

How much do you enjoy being with other people?

How much do you like to party?

How much do you like your family?

The leaders should try to encourage awareness of the other characters.

Hang on, you love money but you don't like working? Is that right? So what do you think about her – she really likes working…

OR

Have you noticed that you two are the only ones who like being with other people? Maybe you like each other? Have you met before?

Following the exercise, those watching should comment on what they have seen: which characters seemed to like each other, which didn't, what kind of group were they (e.g. maybe they all like to party in which case you might think about setting the scene in a town where they love rock and roll; or maybe they all liked family, so you might think about grouping them into families…) and any other observations.

Also ask the performers about any discoveries they made while in the space and any observations they had about the group or the other characters. You can use some of these ideas to help develop your story.

Where might these characters live? (eg a block of flats, the moon, the countryside…)
Did you observe any "groups"? (eg thieves, children, a family, bankers)
When do you think these characters exist?

Character Back-story

This exercise will help you to create a character profile and back-story for the characters and begin to discover the world they are inhabiting.

Following the above exercises, the group should decide on where and when to set the story. If possible, (especially if there are more than 8 characters) identify two distinct groups, then decide on two locations or eras – this can help to give the piece an interesting form, for example modern characters waking up in the middle ages; characters travelling to exotic destinations etc

Having decided on where to set the story, each performer should create a back-story for their character.

Name:

Year of Birth:

Place of Birth:

Age:

Current residence [town, city, place, type of "house"]:

Who do they live with, if anyone?

Are they in love?

What might a typical day be like for them?

Are they connected in any way to the other characters?

Have they ever met any of the other characters? When, where, what happened?

It is best if you can each create your character profile individually and use your time together to improvise with your characters or discuss how the characters can come together in your piece.

Share your character's story and listen to the others' stories to see whether you can find any connections to your own.

CHAPTER 5
CREATING TEXT

Physical Theatre seems at its best when movement and text are integrated. If you are using dialogue you'll need to decide whether you want it to match the style of the piece.

Using Poetic Text

A carefully choreographed sensual movement sequence might be accompanied by poetic text to heighten the beauty of the scene. The language doesn't have to be elaborate and the vocabulary can be simple. But playing with the rhythm of speech can communicate to the audience a state of mind very quickly. For example, long sentences might communicate a lucid state of mind, while short statements might indicate agitation. For fantastic examples of this, see the works of the master of the English language, William Shakespeare.

Here is an extract from ¨Goddess¨, a piece created by Forbidden Theatre Company. This is the first dream the Woman has, where she explores the idea of forbidden love through the story of Psyche and Eros, love between a mortal and a god. Here, Psyche is waiting to be sacrificed to a monster at the top of a mountain. Aphrodite, Goddess of love, jealous of Psyche's beauty, has sent Eros to shoot his love arrows at Psyche, to make her fall in love with the monster.

When Eros is about to shoot one of his arrows at Psyche, he trips and shoots himself, falling in love with her. He takes her away with him making sure that she doesn't actually see him, as he wants to keep his God identity from her.

(EROS spots PSYCHE and gets ready to shoot his arrow. Unfortunately right at that moment he clumsily trips, shoots himself (in the foot) and falls in love with Psyche. Silence. EROS looks at PSYCHE, but she can't see him. EROS goes to Psyche, and unseen by her lifts her off the ground, teaches her to fly (teaches her to love?))

PSYCHE
And then,
A breeze,
A breeze that far from hurting me begins to cradle me....
Then turns into....
A gust of wind, a gentle wind which lifts my feet off the ground
I surrender
A gentle wind.....

(Through the following dialogue, Psyche does not see Eros as he is standing behind her.)

PSYCHE
Who are you?

EROS
That is not for you to know.

PSYCHE
Soft breeze...
Do you love me?

EROS
More than you could imagine.

(He lifts her.)

PSYCHE
Where are you taking me?

EROS
To our home

(EROS takes PSYCHE away from the mountain, saving her from dropping several feet every time she feels unsafe in the air. She tries to hold onto him but slips away, the third time this happens, she is held by the BROTHER, who appears during a sharp intake of breath from all characters, including the WOMAN. The dream freezes, the

woman is not just dreaming of love, she misses her brother's protection. Meanwhile
EROS is holding the image of PSYCHE in his hands (she is still in the
BROTHER's arms.))

PSYCHE
You cradle me,
Far from being scared I feel safe in your arms.
Do you love me?

EROS
More…. More than you can imagine.

PSYCHE
You have given me back my life. I must see who has saved me from….

EROS
No! You mustn't, you must never see who I am. We must love each other
at night, in darkness….

(As the BROTHER passes PSYCHE to EROS.)

PSYCHE
A gust of wind,
A gentle wind which lifts me off the ground
I surrender,
A gentle wind…..

As you can see, the dialogue is kept to a minimum, and is used to pass
detailed information to the audience. For example, "Scared, I am left at
the top of a mountain" immediately tells the audience where Psyche is.
The performer can show by her movement that she is somewhere that is
making her uncomfortable, somewhere where she is cold, from where she
can look down. The text helps her pass specific information on.

Similarly, a carefully choreographed section can depict flying without the
performers lifting their feet off the ground. In ¨Goddess¨, a sequence was

created which gave the illusion of the upper body being lifted, - the rest was done by the text: "A gentle wind which lifts my feet off the ground."

The whole sequence above is performed with the actor playing Eros remaining always behind Psyche.

Through the dialogue

"PSYCHE: Who are you?
EROS: That is not for you to know",

we know that Eros is deliberately remaining out of Psyche´s sight.

Stylising your Speech

If you want to move away from naturalistic text, you can also do this by working through a scene initially improvised in a naturalistic way.

Play the scene in character and communicate vocally as much as you need to and in whatever way comes natural. Keep the scenes short and ask someone else from the group to watch and write down any important moments.

Improvise the scene again, making sure you have given the characters an ACTION to perform either related or unrelated to your piece. For example, they might be arranging a pile of books in alphabetical order. Carrying out a physical action will keep your conscious brain busy, allowing your creative side to work on using language.

Try not to answer any questions directly – for example,

A
Are you feeling all right?

B might answer, instead of "yes":
Is the sky blue today?

So, if you are using movement to tell your story you might consider finding a vocal language which will complement it. Or, if you want to create a comic or quirky effect you can have the characters use naturalistic dialogue in a scene as they carry out abstract movement.

Using a Narrator

There might be instances in which you might want to use a narrator or narrators. For example:

- If the plot is complicated or you have a number of subplots which you want the audience to understand completely.
- If the location varies greatly from piece to piece. This might be more suited to fantastic stories where the action takes place in worlds difficult to depict. "After leaving her castle, the princess found a cave on the opposite shore of the river."
- If time passes in between scenes.
- And more obviously, if you have adapted a story-telling style for your piece.

There are many ways of using a narrator figure – the characters can narrate themselves, or the performers can alternate between their character/s and the narrator. And don't forget that narrator figures can also have very distinct attitudes to the piece, to other characters and to the audience.

CHAPTER 6

STYLISING YOUR WORK

Using a Prop

One of the ways in which you can stylise a scene is by channeling communication between the characters through a prop. The best way of explaining how you can do this is through an example: The Can Scene, from Forbidden Theatre Company's devised show 'Flat One'. This is the first time we meet the characters so you don't need any background information, just as Steve and Ruth didn't have any information on their characters when they created it.

The scene begins with Steve sitting on a "sofa" (two chairs usually signify two chairs, but by magic three chairs become a sofa, or a bench.). Ruth places a can of coke in the middle of the room after she's finished drinking it. Steve removes it. Ruth puts it back. Steve crunches it and throws it away. Ruth tries to restore it to its original shape by blowing into it and puts it back in Steve's view. Steve starts laughing gently to himself – this whole situation is ridiculous. He is apparently trying to make up with Ruth. They start getting "physical" with each other and soon it looks like they are about to have sex on the floor. However this is just a clever manoeuvre by Steve to pick up the can from the floor and chuck it to one side. Ruth is about to give up on the whole can issue when she spots another can at the other side of the room. But so does Steve. They both get ready to dash towards it – as in an Athletics race. They both GO! And Ruth picks up the can. With a victory smile on her face she holds up both cans. Steve looks at her and says "I'm leaving". Ruth is left to bring up two cans on her own.

The whole scene is performed without any words except for Steve's "I'm leaving", which makes the text even more powerful. All the characters' frustrations are channeled through the can of coke – however, the audience understands that the scene is about the breakdown of a relationship as each character tries to get their own way.

The main story is pretty clear: a couple argues, they both try to win until one of them can't take it any more, and leaves. But the absence of text means that each member of the audience will interpret the subtleties of the scene in different ways. This is one of the joys of Physical Theatre.

Stylising an Emotion

Improvise the moment you want to stylise as a one minute naturalistic piece. Once you have done this, set it. Find the exact moment you want to stylise. Usually this will be a change in emotion, so identify the precise moment during which this occurs. Perform the piece again and monitor what your body does during that change in emotion. Be specific. Avoid generalisations like: I am quite relaxed and then I get tense. What is it that your hands do? What about your chest? Your eyes? Your toes?

Share these physical changes with the other people in the group. When you explain things to other people, you force yourself to be clearer and often come up with things you hadn't thought of on your own.

Once you have done this, run the piece again, but this time exaggerate the movements during the moment of stylisation. For example, a small twitch of the forehead will lead to a large frown. Or a small exhalation of breath will turn into a deep sigh. Increase the actions gradually, running the piece over and over again.

As with slow motion, you might want to mark the point at which the stylisation occurs, when the change might become almost a jolt. This shows the audience that something different is about to happen, or something of significance. It also "warns" them that you are about to do something theatrical.

In this way, when you stylise an emotion, you know it is coming from somewhere true from your character. You have allowed the emotion to affect your body and then used these changes to shape it into a more theatrical form.

Using Surrealism

If you need to create more material, go back to your script and see whether there is anything the characters <u>say</u> which the audience could be <u>shown</u>. Do the characters ever talk about their dreams? Their thoughts? What would be more fascinating than seeing the images formed in a character's mind?

A surreal image can help you make your piece more visually interesting and add depth to your piece. For example, there might be a character who is happily telling her friend about something that has happened to her. Her friend knows something is wrong but is not quite sure what. The audience however, can see an alter ego figure physicalising in slow motion the most harrowing emotion. The audience is not only shown what is going on inside the character's mind, but are also invited to feel what the character is feeling.

CHAPTER 7

THE SOUND AND MUSIC

Music can improve the quality of a piece in many ways. It can help INSPIRE YOU in the creation of scenes and developing characters and it can also help to move the audience or create atmosphere. As music speaks directly to the heart without having to be analysed, it can move the audience without them having to analyse intellectually what you are trying to convey.

Be very careful with the type of music you use: well-known tunes are fun and we all enjoy listening to them, but so will the audience. They probably have places or moments they associate with them and it might actually take them away from the piece rather than draw them further in. Soundtracks are often very suitable – again, try and find tracks that are not well known (unless of course you wish the audience to make an association between the film and your piece).

Look for soundtracks from foreign films; look for compilations of film composers or from contemporary composers such as Philip Glass, or Michael Nyman or Zbigniew Preisner. Or of course, should you be lucky enough to have a talented musician in your group, do create your own music.

Remember too that there are many other ways in which you can use your voice besides speaking. The most obvious way that comes to mind is singing, but there is always humming, making noises with your mouth, using the breath. Also clicking fingers, clapping or stomping – creating rhythms and changes in these is also a way to add atmosphere to your piece.

Finding the Mood

There might be a scene which requires one or more characters feeling a strong emotion. It is sometimes difficult to portray this as a performer, especially if the emotion is an unpleasant one, like extreme anger or sorrow. In order to help you portray this, find a piece of music that evokes the emotion you are looking for. Then improvise the scene to the music – it might not involve text and the improvisation need not go on for long.

If you have already set the scene, then try it with music in the background. Take your time, do not rush the scene and make sure you keep the blocking and delivery of the lines spontaneous so that the music can affect you. No matter what the effect of the music on the scene, then play the scene without the music. Again, keep it fluid – the music might have changed something in your original blocking and delivery of the text which is worth keeping. Remember to discuss the effect of the music afterwards with the group – if the music has evoked a strong feeling you might be tempted to immediately decide that the scene works best with music, but remember that an emotional moment can be incredibly potent if played in silence.

Action Against the Music

In the same way as you might wish to use a piece of music to heighten the mood of the scene for an audience, you might want to use music to contrast it. This can sometimes have a comic effect, or even a harrowing one. There is something slightly disturbing for example about watching someone crying their eyes out while REM´s "Shiny Happy People" is playing.

If you are using heavily stylised or choreographed sequences to music, again it might be worth experimenting with going against the tempo of the music. For example, a slow motion fight can go very well with an upbeat tune where fluid movements are used against a very strong disco beat.

CHAPTER 8

THEATRICAL DEVICES

Human Sets

Don't forget that as well as playing characters, you can play inanimate objects. For example, the ensemble can become the mountain one of the characters needs to climb. Or each member can become the piece of furniture of a house.

Whatever you do, there are some things you might like to check out:

- Where is your focus? Are you all staring right ahead of you? Or are you looking at the action? Or are you all looking in different directions? If you are doing this last one, make sure you draw attention to it in some way or else it will look that the performers don't know what they are doing.
- If movement is involved, are you all moving at the same speed?
- Are your bodies holding tension in the same places?
- If you are making sounds, are they synchronized? Or random? Or in a certain order? Is the rhythm in which you make the sounds altered?

As an example, imagine that one of your characters is going on a journey. They have to cross a river, climb a mountain and make their way through a deep forest. The ensemble can help create all these scenarios, fluidly, one after another. But you must make sure that the transitions from one "place" to another are given plenty of attention. This can be very theatrical and you can really wow your audience.

Slow Motion

Slow motion is very useful to highlight moments of importance, to introduce comedy into the piece and to show surreal moments. Here are some things to consider when using slow motion:

- Make sure everyone is moving at the same pace! (Unless for comic effect you want everyone to move at different speeds.)
- Make sure ALL your body parts are moving slowly – you need to dissect your natural movement and then repeat it controlling every single action.
- What is your face doing?
- At what **exact** moment do you all go into slow motion? And when do you change back to normal speed? Don't leave this to chance, set a cue. Also remember there needs to be a change in the body, almost like a jolt, at the instant the slow motion kicks in.

PART 3

WORKING WITH MASKS

"Wearing a mask creates an awareness of 'inner feeling' which accumulates behind the mask and seeks expression through the body."

Dymphna Callery, 'Through the Body'.

CHAPTER 9
INTRODUCTION TO MASK WORK

I have included a brief introduction to mask work in this book, as masks can prove a useful teaching tool and working with them can be liberating for the student. For more on Mask work, including how to make masks, I recommend Toby Wilsher's book 'The Mask Handbook'.

The Power of the Mask

In a world where the Internet rules, where video is available on the phones we carry with us and where we can have the most adventurous experiences at the click of a games console button, why do people continue to make and watch theatre?

A trip to the theatre is a journey into another world: a world of ideas, a world of emotions, a world of magic… Theatre presents a condensed human experience. A good theatre experience will trigger your emotions a few times and leave you feeling like you have just been part of someone else's life.

Whereas television transports us somewhere else by showing us a familiar reality, theatre creates its own reality and seduces us into accepting it. Physical theatre, visual theatre, total theatre, name it what you will, captures our imaginations at different levels and engages us by applying varying doses of surrealism. (It is interesting to note how surrealism has also popped into mainstream television in the past decades eg Ally McBeal, Six Feet Under, Ellie Stone etc.)

When a mask appears on stage, you know you're in a different world. The creature in front of you is not quite human, but it is inhabiting your world. Its face is still and yet full of expression. How can this be?

Your brain picks up clues from the performer's body, without your conscious mind even being aware of it. Your mind is working in a different way – making links that make you see something that is not really there: the mask smiled… well, you <u>think</u> you saw the mask smile.

What you did was register the physical stance and movements of a smiling character, which made you think you saw the mask smile. As an audience you have no choice: you either engage with this type of theatre or you miss out completely on what's happening on stage.

As theatre maker, you place a mask on the stage and BANG! You've transported your audience somewhere else.

The Freedom of Masks

For the theatre-maker and performer, the use of masks opens up a world of possibilities – an ensemble of four can suddenly play a number of characters without the audience recognising each actor by their face; a young actor, through detailed physical work, can play a 75 year-old woman; someone bored of being typecast as the beautiful ingénue can finally become the villain… The list goes on.

Mask can transport us to a land far, far away. Once we have signaled to the audience "we're not dealing with the real world here", we can take them on an epic journey, through rivers, mountains, busy cities – supported by good lighting and appropriate music, the mask can takes us anywhere without leaving the stage.

Safe behind the mask, the actor is likely to be freer to experience a range of emotions. Having to find a different way of working and being "shielded" from the audience by the mask, can help to dive into areas we didn't dare to before.

In his book "Training for the Theatre" Michel Saint-Denis recalls how his uncle Jacques Copeau, began to use masks in rehearsal. One of the actresses he was working with was holding up a rehearsal as she struggled to express her character's emotions in an appropriate physical manner. In an attempt to put an end to her self-consciousness, Copeau threw a handkerchief over her face and asked her to repeat the scene. Her body relaxed at once and she was able to play the scene. And so the mask was used as a training tool for the first time.

But of course this freedom comes at a price: the removal of facial expression and speech from performance.

The Discipline of the Mask

There are many rules to follow when using the mask and these can all be discovered by the student as they experience and observe what works and what doesn't. The first rule to be discovered is: when working with a full mask, you can't speak. When using a half-mask, you can't just use your own voice, you have to find a different one. Not any voice will do, you need to find the voice of the mask.

Whereas television focuses on the face, the mask directs the audience's focus to the body. So relying on facial expressions to convey emotion is no longer possible – which by the way, does not mean that an actor's face stays neutral when working behind the mask. On the contrary, as humans our faces are changed by emotion. The actor's face behind the mask should remain expressive, but the emotions will be channeled through the body.

Masks in Training and Education

The mask will take an audience into a different world and help the actor to connect with their body and find emotional truth.

These are aspects that should be part of all theatre experiences, regardless of the performance style. The mask can therefore highlight their importance and be very useful when training the performer or teaching drama.

The neutral mask in particular, is a wonderful teaching tool – it only comes alive when the actor is fully present and moving with economy. Those watching their fellow students can <u>see</u> what works and what doesn't. Furthermore, it is only through interaction with the rest of the class that the student can learn to use the mask: by gauging their reactions as an audience and receiving verbal feedback when the exercise is over.

47

This process highlights the collaborative aspect of theatre-making and the importance of learning from watching others.

Neutrality, Selflessness and Economy of Movement

"Detached from your own face and words, both of which you can usually master in a social context, the body emerges as the only thing to guide you through the silence and you begin to feel its importance."

Jaques Lecoq, 'Theatre of Movement and Gesture'

Wearing a neutral mask for the first time can have one of two effects (or both!): it can feel liberating to stand in front of an audience hiding behind a mask or it can be incredibly exposing as all you can do is "be there", present, without entertaining an audience through the use of speech or acting tricks.

The neutral mask, expressionless, should help us find a state of neutrality, that "blank sheet" from which we can start to create. The mask highlights mannerisms and accentuates the posture. For those students or performers who have difficulty in connecting to the body, it might help them to alter their posture, to be aware of how they can adjust their stance.

Underneath the neutral mask, the face disappears and the audience takes in the whole body. A small gesture, a slight shift of body weight will become apparent… and important. Too much movement and the audience will just see an actor with a mask – the right gesture, a clean movement and the audience will be moved by the character.

It is important to ease the students slowly into mask work, to allow them to experience each exercise with masks. For some, it will only take a short time for them to express emotion, even to play a situation. Others will discover for the first time that it is possible to communicate without words.

Working in a mask requires both discipline and selflessness – great qualities to nurture in any performer and indeed, in any individual.

The Truth Behind the Mask

To the inexperienced performer, the mask might seem to be a piece of costume, something you put on your face that makes you look different. It is therefore very important to remind the students that the depth of work achieved by working in mask is similar to that of working without it. Assuming that working in a mask only involves wearing it is like assuming that in order to perform a script you just have to read the text. It won't work.

The emotions still need to be true. You still need to play a character. And you still need to communicate with your audience.

The essence of acting in a mask is the same as any other form of acting, you just need to shape your performance in a different way. Using everyday gestures when wearing a mask does not work – you have to find a new performance language. Trying to gesture to replace words does not work either. Any attempt at naturalism will cloud the mask.

Performing in a mask is not cosmetic, only emotional honesty will work. In order for the audience to believe that you are sad, you will need to find a place of sadness. Clouding the emotion with big gestures showing how you remove the tears from your eyes will not work – but an honest sigh which leads to a depression of the chest, might bring a tear to the audience's eyes.

The best work takes place when the performer is fully in character – when the actor is not thinking about what they will do next, they just do it; when they are not thinking: how would my character react? They just react. Similarly, performing with a mask requires this kind of commitment, losing oneself in one's character. For some performers, it might even be easier to make new discoveries behind the mask, where they might find it easier to "let go".

Building a Character

If you or your students are used to creating psychological profiles and back-stories for characters which then feed into the physical performance, then it might be useful to think of the process of working with a mask as the opposite of this.

When working with a mask, and in most physical theatre, the discoveries will be made in the space. To discover our masked character we don't need to think about it, we just wear the mask and remain open to what it suggests; to what our interaction with the audience suggests. Pretty much like with a character, we might not be sure of who this person is we are creating, but just get a sense for it. Then we can experiment with the physicality of the character; we can feel what works best. We can interact with objects, maybe with another mask, with the audience… And following a period of exploration, we can then begin to decide on those aspects of the character that interest us most or that feel 'right'. From here we can build the psychological profile of the character and decide on their back story. We are building a character from the outside in. (The exercises "Interactions" and "Creating a Back-story" in Part 4 are particularly useful for this and can easily be adapted for mask work.)

Simplicity

One of the most challenging aspects of working with a mask is the simplicity required. The mask will only take one thought at a time. This is difficult for a contemporary performer, especially when used to dealing with subtext.

To say that a mask can only carry out a gesture at a time would be simplifying the process. Clarity of thought is what's required.

CHAPTER 10
WORKING WITH MASKS

Here are some exercises to help you and your students get ready to work with masks. Depending on the age of the performers and the depth of the work, some will be more suitable than others. If you are only spending a couple of sessions on mask work, then a good physical stretch followed by an exercise like Grandmother's Footsteps might suffice to get into the spirit of the work. If you are working on masks over a term (or longer) or creating a performance, it is important that you spend about a quarter of the session warming up – this will help the students develop the physical awareness and focus needed for mask work.

A Word on Coaching the Mask.

During mask work, you will need to "coach" the mask, to guide the performer through their thought processes by talking to their character.

The role of the teacher or "mask coach" is essential to help performers develop their characters. Coaching requires detailed observation, focus and imagination, as it will help the performer develop their character in the early stages. Less experienced students will tend to stand in the space not doing much. The mask needs to move in order to become alive and the character behind the mask should be developed primarily in the space – the role of the coach is central to this process.

To help the students build their characters, you will have to pick up on the smallest/subtlest of clues and body language. For example

Hello. Don't you want to step into the space? You like to maintain your distance? Are you observing us? Ah, I think you're making me a bit nervous…. You seem pleased. Maybe you like making people nervous…. I'm not nervous anymore, why don't you try with someone else? Yes, with them… Don't you like them?…

By making suggestions they can react to, you take the pressure away from the student to create. They become less self-conscious as they are splitting the focus with you. They can make spontaneous decisions and movements.

Try to ask closed questions. Open-ended questions like *"Why don't you like her?"* might encourage the student to start gesticulating to express a thought or idea, taking them back into naturalism.

Devising with Masks

One of the beauties of creating a piece of theatre with masks is that the students can be easily encouraged to create through being in the space and watching others, rather than be tempted to sit down and write a script.

Working with masks provides the opportunity to create a new world with characters that interact in ways different to those in the "real world", where speech and facial expression are often the main tools of communication.

Central to the process is the role of the audience/creator. The performer working with the mask will have ideas to build on, but hopefully, their spontaneity will also create new situations, movements and emotions. The audience is there to record these and to make suggestions about how they can develop.

Creating a Character in the Space

Following preparation, ask the Mask to enter the space. There might be a chair in the space. Or a table with a prop.

Welcome the mask.

Hello.

Wait for a response. Depending on the response, ask why they are feeling that way.

You seem a little shy. Are you scared of us? Maybe you just don't like meeting new people. If you're more comfortable maybe you can sit down on the chair. Go on... If you're worried it's dirty, just dust it off with your hand. Is it comfortable? I see from the way you are sitting on it, you are still a bit nervous about talking to us...

Try to pick up on movements, gestures or postures that might indicate a certain emotional state. You can also ask questions about family or background...

Did you get here on your own today? Was it a long journey? Are you tired? Really? How tired? That much? Do you make this journey often? You must be really fed up...

You can go on for as long as you want to or for as long as you think the performer can take it. It is important to let the students know before hand, that depending on what happens in the space, you will take longer with some students than with others and that this has to do with how relaxed the performer is and how suited they are to the mask.

(In medium-large groups, you might want to have two or three masks at the same time.)

After the exercise, ask the performer to take off the mask and tell the rest of the class about any images they saw, or some of the reasons for their behaviour. For example, following the coaching to the mask above, you might want to ask where they were coming from and why they made that journey every day. After a couple of minutes, ask the audience for suggestions to develop the character they have seen. For example, how old do they think the character is, whether they have a family, what job they might be doing etc....

If the group is small, it might be interesting to work with the same mask again, to develop some of the ideas. For example, the mask above can be going on a long journey every day because they take the train, the bus, the tube and then walk to their place of work every morning. You can then ask the performer to show us what that would be like; some of the other students can help by being other passengers, walls of the train, the seats etc....

Further Development

This is also an opportunity to help the performer develop their physicality further, experimenting with different techniques (e.g. the Elements) or simply just by adjusting their posture or movement (e.g. take wider steps to make them prouder; soften the chest to make them humbler).

Following this, you might want to continue developing characters and story through the last two exercises in Part 4.

"PLAYING" IN MASK – Grandmother's Footsteps

When working with masks, Grandmother's Footsteps can also be used to train focus and body awareness. The face is always facing the front, no matter where we are moving, how we are moving, we always face the front as our focus is on grandmother. Spatial awareness becomes very important – I don't need to look at what my limbs are doing, I am SENSING how they move through space.

Through this exercise, the performer can also practice suspension. Suspension is very important for the mask performer – too much movement clouds the audience's perception of what's going on – characters have to give each other focus and every little movement might distract an audience. However, we can't just freeze, or stay still: we have to SUSPEND.

More specifically, Grandmother's Footsteps can also be used to develop the characters in the space spontaneously; to create pictures, ideas and relationships that can be used in a new piece.

Once the students are familiar with the game of Grandmother's Footsteps and they are used to working with masks, they can play the game wearing their masks. You can change stage 2 to create material or ideas for scenes between characters. For example, instead of placing 2 chairs in the space, you can place 3 (recognised symbol for the set sofa) and have the masks lie on it before they can touch Grandma – this might be helpful when building a scene taking place in the living room. Following this, you can add a remote control and make holding it once part of the rules.

Play the game with only five masks, or even three. Explain to your students that they will need to slow down a bit; that they will need to adapt to the mask and find a new way of playing the game. Ask them to let the mask affect how they play but avoid adding any "character or emotions" to the game, or they will miss out on some genuine exploration. Avoid telling them in advance that you might also be creating material for a scene, as they might begin to generate that material in their heads.

Masks are child-like and so the best way to start coaching the masks in this game is when Grandma first turns round. Some of the masks might be scared the first time this happens. Play with that.

What happened there? Did Grandma scare you? She's just playing a game with you. Come, come touch Grandma, you see, she doesn't bite... (To the other mask, who is laughing) You find it funny? Is that because she didn't scare you? Is that because you are older? You've seen it all before haven't you? (To the third mask, who hasn't moved one bit) Wow, look at you, holding that pose, well done... You're really good at this, aren't you? What other poses can you do? I think the next time Grandma turns round, you should try to do something that really shows your ability, like standing on one foot...

Just by playing the game and having Grandma turning once, three different characters have emerged: a naïve/childlike one, a streetwise one and a proud one.

Ask the audience to watch what is happening to the performer's bodies as they play the game, allowing the masks to take over. Every part of the body should be warm and loose and therefore ready to express a variety of emotions. Maybe the child-like character's arm is particularly expressive; or the actor playing "the proud one" is sticking out their chest;

maybe the hips of the actor playing the "streetwise" one have become really loose...

Playing with the mask without worrying about performing, about technique, about creating a character or creating a scene, will make us use our bodies in the most appropriate ways. This is the exploration process: during it, we can make a note (best if our audience makes a note and then feeds back) of what it is that we are doing that rings true; of what is helping the audience through the illusion that the mask has come alive.

So, in the example above, the actor playing the streetwise kid might swing their hips; their weight might be further on their heels than their toes; they might bob their head when they nod. Ideally, the performer will not think of any of this when they work with their mask. However, we are all human and sometimes it takes a while to get inspired. If, at some point in the class or in rehearsal, a performer has trouble getting into character, they can use these three key actions to help their body and minds remember the mask.

The Elements into Mask

You can use the Elements to develop the physicality of the mask characters.

Ask the students to pick one or two elements that are suitable for their characters or that they want to explore further. In small groups, give them some time in the space to explore the movement wearing the mask. Ask them to cross the space, sit down, pick up a chair, an object... Ask them not to worry about the audience, just to play in the space. After five minutes, ask them to make a decision on the element that suits their character best. For the more advanced students you can suggest they choose one element for the top half of the body and a different element for the bottom half.

Work with each student individually. Following coaching instructions similar to those in the exercise Creating a Character in the Space (described at the beginning of this chapter), ask the students to work with the physicality they have chosen. Make sure that they are embodying the element with every part of their body. After a while, suggest a different element for them to work with, to see what happens to their character.

PART 4

FIVE PLAYS TO PLAY WITH

These five pieces were created by a group of theatre practitioners to experiment with different ideas and styles, as part of their continuous professional development. I have put them together so that they can be used by others who wish to explore different theatre styles. Whether you are in love with theatre, or you just want to get together and "play" with some friends or whether you are a teacher in need for material to help your students see that theatre can go beyond the spoken word, these plays are for you.

SO YOU WANT TO BE A PHYSICAL THEATRE PERFORMER?

by Pilar Orti

Introduction

Professor Phillipe Hoffmanonsky, from the LeyCoke Institute of Bodily Mimed Expressive Arts takes us through the characteristics of physical theatre and the qualities of the physical theatre performer. This brief "lecture" takes a comic look at Physical Theatre - the need for slow motion, non-linear structure and much, much repetition...

This is an Ensemble play which will require the performers to act as a chorus. It can therefore be used as an introduction of how the Chorus can be used in modern performance, as well as a brief insight into physical theatre. Brief notes are included to explain some of the concepts in this "lecture".

SO YOU WANT TO BE A PHYSICAL THEATRE PERFORMER?
by Pilar Orti

A lecture in seven freeze frames by Professor Phillipe Hoffmanonsky, from the LeyCoke Institute of Bodily Mimed Expressive Arts

PROFESSOR
Good evening, and welcome to the first series of lectures delivered by Forbidden Theatre Company. Here to help me, are my visual aids, students of the LeyCoke Institute of Bodily Mimed Expressive Arts.

(The students remain motionless, expressionless, the extraordinary representation of NEUTRAL.)

This programme of BODILY lectures has been DEVISED in order to further our Education Programme. Tonight's PIECE addresses the question: why do so many young people in our current society want to be physical theatre performers?

It is important, first of all, to look at the origins of British physical theatre. How this complicated yet emotive art form came to be. Being an horticultural society, it was only a matter of time before this branch of theatre prominent in Europe planted its first seeds in our country.

(Of course during this, the students "become" a tree growing.)

And now it is time to ask: what qualities should one look for in the physical theatre performer? The most important thing to remember is: that although there IS an "I" in Physical Theatre, (one in its written form, two in its spoken form, I being the "EE" in PHY and the "I" in SICAL, and of course there is another EE in THEatre, although this one is only spoken, not written) although there is an "I" in physical theatre, there is no "I" in ensemble, if not, it would be insimbil, or eenseembeel.

The physical theatre performer has no ego, he, or she, must give themselves entirely to his or her craft. Black rehearsal clothes are imperative, to form a true ensemble, where the whole is larger than the sum of its parts. Which neatly leads us to the Chorus.

(The students clump together, like a Greek chorus.)

Ah, the Chorus. It reacts, *(the students act surprised)* it moves as one *(the students move forward together, as one)* and yet, if you watch carefully, you can still see the individual characters coming through *(the students take on individual characters, waving at the audience.)*

The physical theatre performer uses his body as his tool to create Character. The physical theatre performer does not waste his time thinking of the emotional makeup for their new persona. What's more important is how they move: how they walk, how they look, how they scratch their nose. All this allows for instant communication with the audience about the character's state of mind. There is no need therefore to find your character's "motivation" as long as you know its "movilization".

This question of a character's movement leads us neatly, (unusual for a physical theatre piece for there is very rarely a linear narrative and nothing leads neatly from one thing to another) to Running.

(The students run, on the spot of course, in true physical theatre style. They change their actions as the Professor mentions them.)

The physical theatre performer must be Oh-so-fit! They need to run, and jump, walk in different manners, run, and run and run, fall on the floor, bash themselves against the wall, hit themselves.....

And they need to be able to do this at varying speeds.

(The students move in slow motion.)

Slow motion is a very important part of physical theatre. It serves to highlight those important moments which you want the audience to remember. It is a very useful device used by those who are, indeed, devising – unfortunately in this day and age, audiences expect a theatre event to be a certain length. Slow motion can be very handy when a company runs out of creative juices and need to, as it were, flesh up the show.

Then there is The Clown. But of course, Clowns are not part of proper physical theatre.

It is very important, in order to attract a young audience, that at some point in a physical theatre piece, the performers do, "a little dance", to a well-known contemporary track. In order to do this at your own will, and for no apparent reason, the description of your show has to have the word "surreal" in it. Or, should you want to explain to your audience the reason for it happening (which, I would like to reiterate is not always compulsory when working within this genre) I suggest, you say, it was "A DREAM"(mouthed)…

ENSEMBLE
A dream… a dream… a dream…. *(whispering and echoing, while moving around the space, in darkness.)*

PROFESSOR
Thank you. Repetition, Stylised language, especially delivered in a violent manner, is an integral part of physical theatre. To illustrate this, my students have prepared their own adaptation of Federico Garcia Lorca's Bloody Wedding.

GROOM
Mother

(Ensemble as Echo: Mother mother mother.)

MOTHER *(obviously symbolising death):*
Yes?

GROOM
I'm going.

(Echo: Where? Where? Where?)

GROOM
To the vineyard.

(Shock from chorus.)

MOTHER
(under her breath, to the chorus) Not yet….

GROOM
Give me the knife.

(Shock from Chorus. Chorus break out into "The Knife" (different poses))

(They all freeze and a slow motion sequence follows where people kill each other and love each other in many different ways.)

BRIDE
There was no moon the night the poet died.

CHORUS
The moon….. DEATH!

(One of the students comes in, holding a lit lamp.)

GROOM
Mother
I'm going.
To the vineyard.

GROOM
Give me the knife.

(GASP from the Chorus and THE END.)

PROFESSOR
As you can see, the economy of language means that the author's ideas are conveyed in the most pungent manner, hitting the audience in their gut, before they have time to process what they are watching or hearing.

So, not to lose the purpose of this lecture. Why do so many young actors want to go into Physical Theatre? It is not a medium to further a showbiz career. Indeed I always ask my students to leave their ego outside the rehearsal room. The ego lingers around, tries to creep in, but never manages to make it back into the performer's body. Every time you work with a new ensemble, there is a need to develop a new physical language – company members must make sure they are talking the same talk, walking the same walk, miming the same wall. Or indeed, becoming the same wall.

If what you are interested in is developing emotional characters, with deep lives and lots of lines of text, physical theatre is not for you. Indeed, often you will find yourself becoming some inanimate object – your character, will not even have a name. Just "chair" or "section of wall number 1". Physical theatre performers will become large objects, like, a wall….

(The students become a wall and follow the Professor's list.)

PROFESSOR
Or a river, or an ocean….

Or a forest, which can engulf some poor passer by….

But they can also become smaller objects, like chairs, sofas, tables…

(As they become the different objects, the students start fighting, in slow motion of course, and making the accompanying sound effects.)

PROFESSOR
Hey, please, we have a lecture here to finish. Come on! Focus! Focus! Discipline!

(One of the students punches him, music kicks in. as the different students fall on the floor, the lights start dimming, until only the light from the lamp used by "The Moon" earlier is left.)

BLACKOUT

THE END

The Ensemble.

The ensemble is the group of actors in a piece, all of which have parts of more or less equal importance. While in Musical Theatre the ensemble is usually the chorus, in Physical Theatre, the ensemble tends to refer to the full cast.

There is emphasis on "ensemble work" during physical theatre, as importance is placed on the whole piece rather than individual stars or roles. This is of particular relevance if chorus work or configuration mime is used, as you will see later on in the lecture. A piece has an "ensemble feel" to it if all the actors seem to be working well together and being generous to each other.

The Chorus.

The Chorus is a group of people who move and/or speak as one or as if they were one entity. In some pieces of physical theatre you might see clumps of people moving together. The difference between a chorus and an ensemble, is that the actors in an ensemble can work independently of each other and have character parts. For example, the actors playing Romeo and Juliet can be part of an ensemble. (If well directed, even plays with "lead roles" can have an ensemble feel.) Some of the cast from Romeo and Juliet (or all of them) will form the Chorus at the beginning of the play, an entity speaking the prologue.

The Clown.

The physical theatre clown is different to that of the circus clown. Sometimes they wear a red nose but this is not necessary.

The physical theatre clown is a character who wants to please everyone (the audience, mainly) and will go to lengths to do so. "Can you lift that wardrobe?" "Yes!" or "I've heard that you are really good at banging your head on the wall, will you show me?" "Yes!"

As you have gathered, the clown first says "Yes!", whether they should or not and then performs the action.

If they hear you laugh, they will do it again… and again… and again, for your pleasure.

The clown also moves and thinks with the Yes/No rhythm. They are never sure of where they are going. So they will always be late, always get on the wrong bus, end up in the wrong town... Yes, there are many people in real life who are natural clowns.

Surrealism.

Physical theatre performers will use the body in ways that you wouldn't observe in real life. That's the beauty of it, you can go beyond realism.

Federico Garcia Lorca's 'Blood Wedding'

Of course the real title of this play is 'Blood Wedding', you wouldn't expect the Professor to get it right.

The poetry and style of this play allow it to be adapted for physical theatre. As it is, it has some wonderful scenes in Act 3 with characters such as the Moon and Death and a Chorus of Woodcutters.

If you don't mind not being precious with the play, you can also include other chorus scenes to highlight the tragic undertone throughout.

Configuration Mime.

As opposed to the more popular object mime, when someone pretends to use an object that is not there, or stuck behind an imaginary wall, configuration mime involves performers taking on the "role" of an object or part of an object. For example, as in the lecture, all performers can pretend to <u>be</u> the wall (as opposed to miming it). My favourite example is The Haunted House, where performers pretend to be all kinds of objects and furniture in a haunted house: a rug, a chair whose arms strangle you, a lamp etc.

UP THE HILL BACKWARDS

by Richard Mann

Introduction

Charlie is a regular guy who falls in love with a regular girl. But getting the girl of your dreams is not always that easy, especially when your imagination leads you to imagine a murder attempt.

This is a purely visual play. There are only two sentences in the whole piece – everything else is told through action. An underscore can be used to give it the feel of a classic European film.

Written for four actors, this piece requires the performers to abandon the need to use language to communicate and focus on developing the characters and their relationships.

Up the Hill Backwards was turned into a short film by Future Legend in 2004.

UP THE HILL BACKWARDS

by Richard Mann

A physical piece of theatre for 4 actors: to music.

CHARACTERS

The Guy

The Girl

The Friend

The Waiter

A Couple - made up of a Girl and a Bloke

Another Bloke

Scene 1.

The Café.

The Girl walks in. Looks around. Finds a table, sits down. The Waiter takes her order.

The Friend enters, looks around, sees The Girl. She goes to her table, they embrace each other, then sit down at the table.

The Waiter is serving, calling out to chef and constantly brings drinks and food out.

The waiter carries a *large knife*, which he uses to cut up pizza, bread etc.

The girls are chatting and laughing loudly. The scene is very busy.

The Guy walks in and crosses the stage, the girls and waiter look at him. He turns round and they all look away. He crosses back to the other side, yet again they all look at him, he turns round, they look away. He crosses once again, this time when he looks around The Girl is staring at him, *a moment.*

She beckons him over, then writes out her number on a piece of paper, she hands it to him then gestures him to phone her. Happily he nods and walks off, only to realise he's going the wrong way. He turns to see the two girls and waiter looking at him, fumbles and exits off the other side. Lights down.

Scene 2.

The Mirror.

The Girl walks into the toilets, looks around for anyone else, then satisfied, she goes over to the mirror (in front of audience), places her bag down on table, opens it and starts to apply make-up in an over the top fashion.

The Friend enters and The Girl cranes her head to look at her. They stand facing each other, tilting their heads from left to right checking each other out.

The Girl circles The Friend in a bitchy way. Then there is stand off, with The Friend being first to draw. Suspense Western style.

Both then apply make-up in an over the top frantic way. When finished there is a *beat*. Then both embrace each other, lots of laughter and *oooo's and Ahhhh's*. Both then go over to mirror; with The Friend opening a slightly larger bag. There is a subtle look from both as she is opening her bag and then when The Girl opens her *smaller* bag. Both put on make up. Once they are ready, they all exit together.

Lights down.

Scene 3.

The Cinema.

A row in a cinema. The film has already started. A Girl and a Bloke come in and take their seats. The Guy and The Girl come in, having to squeeze past the other two. The focus is very much on their *first date.*

All sit facing forward as if looking at the screen. Girl looks at The Guy then at her boyfriend (The Bloke) who swaps seat with her.

Audience reactions; something funny, then even funnier, then scary (The Guy reacts really over the top by jumping onto the chair), the other couple react to him.

Bloke on stage right of The Guy farts, reactions of suppressed laughter from that couple, then looks of disgust from them and The Girl towards The Guy. The Bloke then puts his arms around his girlfriend and The Guy. Looks from The Guy and The Girl, then look to Bloke who reluctantly takes his arm away (wondering what the problem was).

The Guy stares at the girl lovingly (puppy eyes); she gives him a *'what are you doing?'* look. He then puts his hand on her leg. *Beat,* she places it back. Subtly he tries to put his arm round her shoulder, stretching arms forward, then up, then knocking her head side wards.

He gets up from seat apologising to her, falls backwards onto bloke's lap, who pushes him off. Ends up on his hands and knees in front of the girl, *a look.* Travels backward out of the seating, apologising to everyone as they are all looking at him. Lights down.

Scene 4.

The Dejection.

The guy walks away from cinema, downtrodden, he trips over something, *a look*. Stops centre stage and posture falls with an out-breath. Walks to bench, dusts off mess on it, sits down, puts hand on chewing gum. A Mosquito buzz's, The Guy follows it with his eyes, claps at it mid-air, it stops. It starts to rain, he puts his hood up.

A Bloke comes along, sheltering from the rain and sits beside him, *a look*. Stops raining, they both pull their hoods down, *a look*. Music stops.

GUY:
Women!

BLOKE:
Don't you just want to kill them sometimes!

Music resumes. Both of them get up, the Bloke walks off. The Guy looks forward seriously thinking about what the Bloke said, he closes his eyes...

Scene 5.

The Dream.

The Guy imagines that he is with The Girl, she walks on, stands by the side of him and places *her head onto his shoulders*. He goes to touch her head. Headwaiter comes on and takes her hand and pulls her away. She has disappeared and when he looks up he can see the waiter with *the large knife,* above her head, leering at him. He rubs his eyes and when he opens them they have both disappeared.

The Guy walks away, downtrodden, he trips over something, *a look.*

Lights down.

Scene 6.

The Café.

Repeat of the first scene. The Guy is standing at the side furtively looking at all the action from behind a newspaper.

The Girl and The Friend have arrived, they are sitting at their table. The Waiter is about to serve them pizza.

The Guy, remembering his dream, thinks that the Waiter is going to try to kill The Girl. Music stops. He lunges at The Waiter in slow motion, screaming at him in a battle cry way *'AAHHHHH!'*, to stop him. He tackles him to the ground. They roll over with a deep *'Thud'*, sounded by The Guy.

Then he makes a heart beat noise.

There is a pause as the girls all look in shock at The Guy. The Waiter is confused and dazed. The Guy gets up realising his mistak. The Waiter lunges for him and starts shouting and chasing him. Music and action resume.

The Guy runs round the back of the chairs, circling them. As he passes the girls one of them joins in chasing. The second time around the other girl joins in. They all run off.

Lights down.

BLACKOUT.

THE END

CAIRO 1948

by Phillip Johnson and Pilar Orti

A short two-hander. Part film noir, part melodrama, *Cairo 1948* is the story of a man and a woman who fall in love only to discover they are both on different sides of the law.

Cairo 1948 is set in a bar in Cairo, in a jeep in the desert, another bar in Nairobi and the jungle in Thailand and spans two decades. Quite a challenge for two performers.

CAIRO 1948

by Phillip Johnson and Pilar Orti

Scene 1

MAN
Cairo 1948. The war was just over. I was in a bar. Drinking. On my own. And then I saw her. There she was, standing, next to her mike. Singing.

(The damsel sings.)

MAN
I watched her sing. She could really sing.

When she ends her singing:

MAN
Would you like a drink?

WOMAN
Yes.

MAN
That's a lovely singing voice.

WOMAN
Thank you.

MAN
Would you like another drink?

WOMAN
Yes.

MAN
Time passed.

WOMAN
Take me out of here. Take me away from all this. The routine. The singing. Take me away from it all.

MAN
So I did. The next day we set off on a journey. In my jeep. But when we got to the frontier.... Oh no. The guards. We can't go there.

WOMAN
Why not?

MAN
I… I never told you what I did for a living.

WOMAN
Does that matter. Is it relevant to our…. Love?

MAN
I…. I smuggle illegal arms. To the rebels.

WOMAN
No!

MAN
She battled with her thoughts. Half of her wanted to stay with me. The other half…. Didn't. She stepped out of the jeep.

MAN
Where are you going? Get back here. You'll never survive out there in this heat.

WOMAN
The soldiers can protect me!

MAN
From that day on, I knew I could never again look her in the eye.

Scene 2

MAN
Nairobi. 1968. The smuggling industry was on the decline. With better customs, the African countries were doing the smuggling themselves. I went to a bar. And there she was. Singing. Oh how she could sing.

She was singing about us. Around her, the tables were full of soldiers. I could see by the way they were looking at her, that she'd been around.

WOMAN
Then I saw him. He was looking at me in… that way he had of looking at me. What I wanted to do was…….

(She throws herself into his arms.)

WOMAN
Oh darling! I have been waiting for you to come back. I know that what you do is not very noble but…. Oh teach me how to smuggle! Teach me how to traffic in arms! *(They waltz.)*

WOMAN
But all I did was….

(She continues singing.)

MAN
I couldn't look her in the eye.

Scene 3

WOMAN
Thailand. 1970. The Guerrillas were about to knock out the current government. It was hot. I was wearing my camouflage gear and was carrying two rifles, in each hand. And then in the distance….. I thought I saw someone I recognised.
Is that…? It all came flashing back. I was in that bar again. Singing…….
And he was back at the bar….. offering me a drink…….. But the reality wasn't as glamorous. I was in the middle of the jungle fighting for survival. The guerrillas needed their arms and I was there to provide them.

MAN
The government was looking for the rebels. I had left my smuggling job and was now employed by the CIA to look for those who were illegally defying the state. And then…. And then I saw her. Carrying two rifles… in each hand. It all became clear, when I was reading the brief, the profile of the leader of this smuggling ring, I couldn't get her out of my head… and now I knew why.

WOMAN
You….

MAN
I…. Am….

WOMAN
I'm sorry…

MAN
I'm sorry too…… and in the middle of all this, gunfire…… the rebels approaching…. A stray bullet……. And her……. Dying in my arms……….

(They dance the waltz.)

BLACKOUT.

THE END

LEGACY IN BLOOD

by Mark Reid

Introduction

Written mainly as a monologue, *Legacy in Blood* begins with a dark ritual, where a woman is offered as a sacrifice to the revered… Mark. An unlikely person to be worshipped, Mark tells us the story of how he discovered he was… how shall we put it, not quite human.

This piece requires a performer who can show the character's vulnerability as well as his darker force.

LEGACY IN BLOOD

by Mark Reid

(The High Priest enters the stage mumbling an incantation. Off stage a discordant chorus sing. As High Priest stands downstage facing audience, the singing stops. Two people enter from upstage wings. One carries a black book, the other a knife. They take up position behind High Priest and hand him the items. High Priest opens the book, holds the knife and recites.)

(Music.)

HIGH PRIEST
Guardians of the East, whose element is air: blow away the veil that separates us from the world of darkness. We summon you to witness our rites and to guard the circle.

(High Priest moves clockwise to the side of the stage and is followed by the duo.)

Guardians of the south whose element is fire: who forges passion and desire in your flames, we summon you to witness our rites and to guard the circle.

(The group moves upstage.)

Guardians of the west whose element is water: out of whose depths life dwells eternally, we summon you to witness our rites and to guard the circle.

(Group moves stage left.)

Guardians of the North whose element is earth: by seed, root, stem and bud, bring us to stand on thy hill of vision. We summon you to witness our rites and to guard our circle.

(Having cast the circle, High Priest takes centre stage holding the knife. He is flanked either side by his two acolytes. Acolyte 1 moves to the side of the stage and opens a door. Human Sacrifice enters in a trance and kneels before High Priest.)

Child of Darksome and divine,
Here we are to call ye forth!
We offer this sacrifice to you,
O prince of death and resurrection.
May this be the day of you sinful re-birth,
As we baptise you with the sweet eternity of life's legacy.
Pass among the shades and shadow of the night.
Move unseen among your enemies by day.
Come to us, your children, who accept you,
As if you were our own blood.

(High Priest cuts Human Sacrifice's throat. The acolytes pull red ribbon from the neck of the victim as the body slumps to the floor.)

(Music finishes.)

Pause.

(The door slowly opens and Mark crawls out rather un-elegantly. He stands before the worshipers, looking at each one, they leave. Mark walks down stage. He appears uncomfortable in the limelight.)

MARK
I've not always been this popular!

(Acolyte 1 and Acolyte 2 come back on stage to remove the body.)

MARK
In fact for most of my life I've not been popular at all. I've always found it difficult to make friends; I was a bit of a loner at school. I remember being jealous of the other kids at school whose parents read them bedtime stories at night. My parents never did that for me. I used to think it was because they didn't like me. But now I think they were just frightened of me. I think it was hard for them, not just because of me, but …they never really loved each other.

In 1983, I was 13! *A beat.* 1983 was a frozen summer. It sits in my mind, crystal clear, as if carved in ice. The emotions that separated my parents are as real to me today as they were then. That summer when my parents hearts froze. *A beat.* And silence. I really learnt the meaning of silence then. It ruptured from beneath our living room carpet. The carpet was white, shag pile and smelt like eucalyptus fabric softener, and when I was little I'd roll around on it pretending I was on the back of a giant sheep. I would look up into an imaginary sky and watch flocks of galahs and cockatoos dart and swoop like wayward firecrackers. That year the carpet lost its warm embrace. The fibres froze and turned to snow.

It was worse at night, the silence I mean. My parents sat in separate lounge chairs either side of it. A huge, invisible wall of silence. When it got bored of them it drifted down the hallway to find me. I could never concentrate on my homework; all I could hear was the screaming silence. It smelt fusty like the old photographs we kept in a shoebox in the attic. *A beat.* I told Father Shane, my school chaplain about it. He said I was just discovering that my parents were 'human'. *A beat.* I don't think he was right. I think it was probably the pair of other woman's knickers my mother found in the back seat of our car.

(Mark shuffles his feet on the floor. He looks as if he has run out of things to say.)

MARK

It was soon after that summer that mum told me I was adopted. It sounds weird, but I totally accepted it. I think I was relieved! I mean the idea of adoption wasn't completely alien to me. Giorgio, the foreign exchange student in my class, who once picked me for his side in footy; he was adopted! And we sponsored a girl in Africa, Sahwila. We used to keep a picture of her on our fridge. She had a swollen belly like a brown balloon, skeleton arms and the longest, softest eyelashes I had ever seen. She drew us a picture of a donkey once. Anyway, that was kind of like adoption. *A beat.* And my sister had a cabbage patch kid.

It was on a Thursday evening, she told me. We'd had torrential storms and smell of damp earth clung to the air. I'd just finished watching 'Buck Rogers' when mum came into my room.

I'll always remember the way mum told me. She used to be in her college debating team, so she had a way with words: 'That lazy, lying, cheating shit I'm married to isn't your father.'

And then she told me about my father, my REAL FATHER!

My real father wasn't the assistant manager of an electronics store. My father lived in the darkness of the night. My real father WAS the night. He was a powerful warrior who commanded an army of loyal men into bloody battle. He ruled over a kingdom whose people trembled at his very name. And if anyone said anything against him or teased him, them he ordered his army into the woods to chop down all the trees. They'd chop off all the braches and remove the bark. Them he'd grab his enemy and after greasing the spiked trunk with his spit, he'd stick it up their bottom, then out their mouth. And he'd put it in his front garden as a warning.

And my dad had special powers! He had command of the animals. He could talk to wolves. Make spiders do his bidding. And cats were his messengers!

But when you're that powerful, that special, people are jealous. And one day they're going to catch up with you. My dad knew he needed a son to carry on his legacy.

Then my mother whispered, as if she were drunk on the very word she was speaking. She whispered my father's name! And she had the most beautiful smile, one I'd never seen before.

As I heard his name my stomach turned inside out with dread and in my mind's eye, his face leered from the shadows. I heard my blood bubble up into my ears, I jumped off my bed and ran outside! I heard it before. My dad was famous. I'd seen films about him, read comic books about him; I even had a doll of him! I felt powerful, invincible. I jumped on the trampoline. *Mark re-lives the moment.* I looked up into the sky, and the night had changed. It was no longer a black lid sealing me into the world; confining me to this family, which suffocated me with their silence. I was free. *A beat.* The night sky glittered suddenly!

(Music.)

(Acolyte 2 enters the stage; she is manipulating a belt, perhaps like a snake. It slithers over to Mark, up his leg, and fastens itself onto his waist. A dinner shirt is manipulated by High Priest and Acolyte 1, some kind of monster! Mark and the shirt fight, during the battle the shirt is dressed onto Mark. Finally a black cape flies onto the stage it envelops Mark, and fastens itself onto him.

As Acolyte 1 goes to leave after putting on the cape Mark hypnotises her. She goes towards him willingly. Mark cradles her, and then takes a lunge towards her neck. Stopping short, he remembers something. Reaching into his pocket he takes out a pair of plastic 'dress up' fangs, puts them in his mouth, then sinks them into her neck. The woman faints/dies.

Music finishes.)

MARK
My father so loved the world, that he gave his only begotten son, that whosoever believeth in him should not perish, but have ever lasting life.

(The woman turns her head towards the audience, her eyes 'snap' open.)

MARK
I am the son of Dracula!

BLACKOUT.

THE END

SOFTLY, SOFTLY

by Pilar Orti

Introduction

This allegorical piece is set in a small village, where there is a strong community feeling. Until one day the villagers loose the ability to speak. The disappearance of the voice brings the breakdown of all communication between the villagers and the joy disappears from everyday life.

Softly, Softly is an Ensemble piece with seven (+1) characters (the +1 character only appears for a few minutes although their role is pivotal).

The piece uses repetition and a voiceover to give it a parable/fairy tale feeling and the actors are required to use the space in an imaginative way to create the atmosphere of a busy market. Mime is also required.

SOFTLY, SOFTLY

by Pilar Orti

Prologue

VOICEOVER
Once upon a time, in a land far, far away, there was a little village. Its market was a vibrant place, the site where everyone greeted each other in the mornings, the place where they all reminded themselves of how close a community they were.

(Music starts.)

Scene 1

(ALEX, the stall owner, and PAULA, his new assistant, come in, setting up two tables in the market.)

ALEX
This table goes here. This other one, there. Now the crates. Apples. Bananas.

PAULA
Apples, bananas. *(Practising)* You'd like an apple? Apples. Bananas.

ALEX
And here we have the Pears and Plums.

(He goes off to get the scale.)

PAULA
Apples, bananas, pears and plums.

ALEX
(coming in on the last beat of the list.) Scale.

PAULA
Apples, bananas, pears, plums, scale.

ALEX
Good.

(GEORGE, the artist, enters.)

GEORGE
Good morning!

ALEX
Lovely Day!

GEORGE
(to PAULA) Good morning?

PAULA
Hi!

ALEX
Your usual...

GEORGE
Apple.

ALEX
(As he picks up an apple and throws it to him.) Apple.

GEORGE
Thanks! *(He sets up his drawing.)*

(SIVE, a young girl, comes in.)

SIVE
Good morning!

ALEX
Lovely Day!

ALEX *(to PAULA)*
And we keep the cash here...

(PRISCILLA, another girl comes in.)

PRISCILLA
Good morning!

ALEX
Lovely Day!

(The girls start skipping. ALEX continues explaining to PAULA how everything works.)

(ERICA and MARK enter. They are an elderly couple.)

ERICA
Good morning!

MARK
Good morning!

ALEX
Lovely day!

(MARK and ERICA walk towards GEORGE and place themselves to each side of him.)

ERICA (to GEORGE)
And what are you drawing today?

GEORGE
Well, see this shape here...

(He is interrupted by:)

ALEX
Ladies and gentlemen...

(All look at Alex, frozen in expectation.)

ALEX
The market is now open!

(They all rush to the market)

GEORGE
(As Erica walks to the stall.) Get me an apple will you love?

(A choreographed sequence starts, where Alex and Paula serve the rest of the villagers.)

(The people are served, the girls leave.)

MARK
Come on dear.

ERICA (to GEORGE):
Here's your apple…

GEORGE
Thank you love!

PAULA and ALEX start to pack up, GEORGE leaves. ALEX stops in the middle of the space.)

ALEX
Now that really was a lovely day!

(Lights down.)

Scene 2

A new day.

ALEX and PAULA set up the stall.

PAULA
Apples, bananas, pears and plums. Scale.

(GEORGE enters)

GEORGE
Good morning!

ALEX
Lovely Day!

PAULA
Hi!

ALEX
Your usual…

GEORGE
Banana.

ALEX
(As he picks a banana and throws it at him.) Banana.

GEORGE
Thanks! *(He sets up his drawing.)*

(SIVE comes in.)

SIVE
Good morning!

ALEX
Lovely Day!

PAULA
Hi!

PRISCILLA *(coming in)*
Good morning!

ALEX
Lovely Day!

PAULA
Hi!

(The girls start skipping.)

ERICA
Good morning!

MARK
Good morning!

ALEX
Lovely day!

PAULA
Hi!

(MARK and ERICA walk towards GEORGE and place themselves to each side of him.)

ERICA (to GEORGE)
And what are you drawing today?

GEORGE
Well, see this shape here…

(He is interrupted by:)

ALEX
Ladies and gentlemen…

(They all look at Alex, frozen in expectation.)

ALEX
The market is now open!

(As Erica walks to the stall:)

GEORGE
Get me an apple will you love?

(The people are served, the girls leave.)

MARK
Come on dear.

ERICA *(to GEORGE)*:

Here's your apple…

GEORGE:
Thank you love!

(PAULA and ALEX start to pack up, GEORGE leaves.)

ALEX's *last line is*:
Now that really was a lovely day!

(Lights down.)

Scene 3

A new day.

(ALEX and PAULA set up the stall.)

PAULA
Apples, bananas, pears and plums. Scale.

(GEORGE enters)

GEORGE
Good morning!

ALEX
Lovely Day!

PAULA
Hi!

ALEX
Your usual…

GEORGE
Plum.

ALEX
(As he picks up a plum and throws it to him.) Plum.

GEORGE
Thanks! *(He sets up his drawing.)*

(SIVE comes in.)

SIVE
Good morning!

ALEX
Lovely Day!

PAULA
Hi!

PRISCILLA
(As she enters.) Good morning!

ALEX
Lovely Day!

PAULA
Hi!

(The girls start skipping.)

ERICA
Good morning!

MARK
Good morning!

ALEX
Lovely day!

PAULA
Hi!

(MARK and ERICA walk towards GEORGE. Mark SR, Erica SL.)

ERICA *(to GEORGE)*
And what are you drawing today?

GEORGE
Well, see this shape here...

(He is interrupted by:)

ALEX
Ladies and gentlemen...

(They all look at Alex, freeze in expectation.)

ALEX
The mar....

(His voice goes. He hasn't really realised he didn't speak, only notices that people are looking at him funny. He "says" again: the market is now open.)

(Everyone looks at each other. No one says a word.)

PAULA
Apples? Bananas? Pears? Plums?

(Realising that ALEX is not going to say his usual words, they follow the assistant's cue, and begin their usual routine. The buying actions are repeated, with a little bit of weariness as something is not quite right and they don't know how to treat Alex.)

(As Erica walks to the stall:)

GEORGE
Get me an apple will you love?

(The people are served, the girls leave.)

MARK
Come on dear.

ERICA *(to GEORGE)*
Here's your apple…

GEORGE
Thank you love!

(PAULA and ALEX start to pack up, GEORGE leaves.)

(ALEX and PAULA stop where Alex would have said, "That really was a lovely day". He starts mouthing "That really was…." And stops.)

(They leave.)

Scene 4

(ALEX and PAULA set up the market.)

(GEORGE comes in.)

GEORGE
Good morning!

PAULA:
Hi!

(ALEX gestures Hi!, makes a gesture which says, your usual?)

(GEORGE is not quite sure how to react.)

(ALEX throws him a pear.)

GEORGE (to PAULA)
Tell him thanks.

PAULA
Thanks.

ALEX (mouths, with no voice)
I can hear.

(SIVE comes in.)

SIVE
Good morning!

PAULA
Hi!

(ALEX gestures "Hi".)

PRISCILLA
Good mor…..

(Her voice goes)

(She repeats "Good morning!" Cheerfully as if nothing had happened, but no sound comes out. Wanting to ignore what's happened, she starts skipping (kind of) and joins Sive.)

(ERICA and MARK enter.)

ERICA
Good morning!

MARK
Good mor….!

(His voice goes.)

(He tries again.)

(ERICA starts the routine again.)

ERICA
Good morning!

MARK
(Mouths good morning, but nothing comes out......)

PAULA
Apples, bananas, pe....

(She too loses her voice and mouthes "...and plums". She tries again, Apples etc, nothing comes out.)

(All half frozen, not sure what to do.)

(MARK and ERICA walk towards GEORGE. MARK SR, ERICA SL.)

ERICA *(to GEORGE)*
And what are you drawing today?

GEORGE
Well, see this shape here...

ERICA
Yes...

SIVE *(joining them)*
Yes....

GEORGE
It's meant to be a curve but at the end it goes into a sharp line

ERICA
Yes...

SIVE
Yes....

GEORGE
But here, where the blue is...

(He waits, thinking that Erica has lost her voice, but she just doesn't know that she is meant to say "yes".)

ERICA
Yes...

SIVE
Y...

(Loses her voice as before she says yes…)

(They all look at SIVE who looks terrified…)

GEORGE
(Hesitant) Well, the blue becomes green and the yellow becomes red and….

ERICA
Carry on dear, I find it all very interesting, I was once an artist myself you know, I used to…

(She loses her voice.)

(GEORGE gets up, terrified, as everyone can't speak except him.)

GEORGE

And when the red becomes white then you really get an image, a floor picture as we call it…

(He loses his voice, only he carries on as though he can still be heard. It's quite disturbing.)

(GEORGE leaves.)

(They all start to leave, one by one.)

(Lights down.)

Scene 5

VOICE OVER
Soon no one in the village had a voice. Time passed.......

(An attempt to repeat the usual sequence. ALEX and PAULA set up. GEORGE comes in. Kind of says "Hi". ALEX gets the fruit ready but as he goes to throw it to GEORGE, GEORGE has already turned round and is about to get to work. The fruit falls on the floor. The girls come in. The old couple comes in. ERICA goes to GEORGE, but MARK stays near the stall. ALEX goes round telling everyone individually that the store is open – first he goes to the girls, then ERICA and GEORGE. MARK tries to get PAULA's attention. MARK is almost knocked over by ALEX as he returns to the stall. As the bump happens, everyone else gets stuck in their movement, repeating a short sequence.

MARK wants an apple, he gestures to ALEX, etc. Finally ALEX gives him the fruit. MARK pays ALEX.

The girls confuse PAULA, she puts some fruit in the bag and gives it to PRISCILLA.

ERICA walks around GEORGE and asks him if he wants a fruit. She walks to the stall. As she gets to the stall, the focus goes to the girls and PAULA.

PAULA finishes handing over fruit to PRISCILLA, puts fruit in another bag for SIVE and begins to do her sums. (MARK is leaving)The girls run away. PAULA about to tell them how much, she tries to shout after them.

ERICA about to pay. PAULA gestures to ALEX that the girls have left, he tries to shout but can't (!), then runs after them. ERICA confused. ALEX comes back. Him and PAULA upset. ERICA confused, leaves without paying, leaves without giving GEORGE his fruit. ALEX leaves, GEORGE upset without food. Goes up to PAULA, she shrugs and GEORGE takes an apple. Exeunt.

Lights down.)

Scene 6

(MARK and ERICA enter. ALEX enters. They look at each other – they are thinking about what to say. They lower their eyes. Cross over.

SIVE enters, PAULA enters with her crates, Priscilla enters, the criss-crossing continues.

At one point they are all in the space. They repeat a small movement, continuously, as if they were stuck in their own little routine.

PAULA walks by with the crates. SIVE tries to call out, can't, follows her. ERICA follows SIVE, PRISCILLA finds bank note that Erica dropped, shouts at her, decides to keep it, leaves the other way.

ALEX and MARK in a diagonal, lift their gaze, locked, begin to walk towards each other, not quite sure what to say, what to do.

A TOURIST enters, with a map

They all freeze and look at him/her.)

TOURIST
Excuse me, I'm about to run out of petrol, my car's just there and I'm trying to follow this map, where do I need to turn to get here?

(ALEX and MARK look at each other.)

TOURIST
I'm sorry to inconvenience you…

(ALEX and MARK half smile. They look at GEORGE, at each other and complicitly walk with GEORGE, guiding him to where he needs to go. The previous sequence where everyone ignored each other takes place again, only this time they begin to make eye contact with each other and interact.)

Through their interaction, they begin to feel like a community again. They guide The Tourist off stage.

To music.)

BLACKOUT.

THE END

FURTHER READING

Through the Body
by Dymphna Callery

A good overview of what is going on in the contemporary world of UK physical theatre. A lovely mixture of practical games and exercises, theory, reflection and some history. A whole chapter on Devising too!

The Mask Handbook
by Toby Wilsher

Written by one of the founders of Trestle Theatre Company, this book covers everything you need to know to create your own mask play. From mask making, through technique and tips on creating your own piece.

The Space to Move: Essentials of Movement Training
by Christian Darley

A beautiful book written by a practitioner completely in love with her subject and her students.

Full of anecdotes and exercises used in actor training that will be useful for anyone interested in how to remain connected to the body in performance. A great advocate for giving us all the space to create.

For more on devising and physical theatre, visit
http://devisingandphysicaltheatre.wordpress.com

ABOUT THE AUTHOR

Pilar Orti was Artistic Director of Forbidden Theatre Company for over ten years. During that time she built an Education Programme together with Linda Baker, designed to inspire the creation of highly theatrical work and build long-term relationships with schools. Through these partnerships, the company took part in high-profile events such as the School Proms at the Royal Albert Hall (with Emma Davies and students from Orleans Park School).

Pilar now runs a learning company, Unusual Connections, focused on leadership training, team facilitation and wellbeing, using everything she learnt as both workshop leader and "manager of people" during her time at Forbidden.

ACKNOWLEDGEMENTS

Thanks go to everyone who, at some point, believed in the strength of the Ensemble at Forbidden, especially to Mark Reid and Richard Mann (contributors to this book), Steve Brownlie, Ruth Hutchinson, Tracey Hammill, Alex Perkins, Pilar Garces, Linda Baker (vital to the company's survival) and of course, Phillip Johnson, without whom Forbidden would have never existed.

Printed in Great Britain
by Amazon.co.uk, Ltd.,
Marston Gate.